the Institute of Management

FOUNDATION

The Institute of Management (IM) is at the forefront of management development and best management practice. The Institute embraces all levels of management from students to chief executives. It provides a unique portfolio of services for all managers, enabling them to develop skills and achieve management excellence.

For information on the benefits of membership, please write to:

Department HS
Institute of Management
Cottingham Road
Corby
Northants NN17 1TT
Tel. 0536 204222

This series is commissioned by the Institute of Management Foundation.

CONTENTS

We are all professionals in the jobs that we do. Yet when it comes to writing, we tend to approach the task in the same old amateur way that we used at school.

Most of us are unaware of the strategies and techniques used by an increasing number of professional writers. Yet, if we wish to make our business writing more effective, there are many things we can learn from the professionals.

By working through this book, you will, in a week, know how to improve both the quality and the speed of your writing. For, by working systematically, you can achieve useful savings in time.

Here, you will learn how to do this step by step each day. The main steps are:

The steps to effective business writing

Sunday	Analysing our writing
Monday	The WRITER'S Strategy – Work, Recitation, Incubation, Treatment
Tuesday	The WRITER'S Strategy – Execution
Wednesday	The WRITER'S Strategy – Revision, Submission
Thursday	Effective letter writing
Friday	Effective report writing
Saturday	Other forms of writing

Analysing our writing

At the beginning of the process of improving our writing skills, we need to know three things:

The starting point

- Where are we?
- How do we find this out?
- What will that tell us?

We need some way of measuring what we do now when we write, so that we can identify some ways of making the task easier, quicker and yet more effective.

We need a method of analysing our own writing.

It is easy enough to pass what we have written over to someone else for comment and this can, indeed, be very useful. But what if there is no one else available at the time we need them? It will clearly be useful to have some means of assessing for ourselves the effectiveness of what we have written.

Fortunately, such means exist; all we need to do is to work through the following:

Analysing our writing

- producing a sample for analysis
- qualitative analysis
- quantitative analysis
- what these tell us

Producing a sample for analysis

It is best at this point to produce a fresh sample of your writing for analysis. You can, if your time is at a premium, use a piece you have already written. If, however, someone else has seen and commented on or edited it, this will not tell you very much about your own unaided writing.

To carry out this exercise properly, get pen and paper together, or place yourself at your word processor. Set aside 20 minutes in which to write a short report or a letter on a subject of your own choice.

For those who cannot easily think of a suitable subject, here are ten topics to select from:

- a short report on your career to date
- a letter to a newspaper about your firm's achievements
- a letter to a business colleague about a new project
- a short report on your department's workload
- a short report on your staff's recent performance
- a letter complaining about poor service received
- a short report on your last assignment or job
- a letter to a subcontractor about poor work
- a short report on your latest idea for improving productivity
- a letter of apology to a complaining customer

The objective is to produce 100–200 words for analysis. Since the average person, writing longhand, can write at about 30–40 words per minute, this should not be difficult within the time.

Write in sentences and paragraphs. Lists or tables of figures will not be suitable for one of the methods of analysis we shall use.

It would be a good idea not to read beyond this point until after you have finished writing. Allow yourself 20 minutes only. Begin as soon as you are ready.

Qualitative analysis

Check through what you have written to make sure you are reasonably happy with it. Now let us analyse what you have produced.

Did you plan what you were going to do before you did it? Did you write this plan down for reference? Or did you just begin writing and make it up as you went along?

You can count it as a plus if you did a plan; a minus if you started writing as soon as your time began.

Does your report have a title or your letter a heading to indicate to the reader what it is about? Plus for a heading or title; minus if you do not have one.

Do your paragraphs all contain sentences which relate to the same topic or aspect of a topic? Or do you have more than one topic per paragraph? A plus for one topic per paragraph; a minus for more than one.

If you have written a report, have you used headings to identify the various sections of the report? A plus if you have; a minus if you have not.

If you have written a letter, do the opening and closing match each other? That is, if you began 'Dear Sir/Madam' did you end 'Yours faithfully'? If you began 'Dear Mr/Mrs/Ms X' did you end 'Yours sincerely'? Plus if you did; minus if you did not.

If you wrote a report, is there a short summary section (usually at the beginning) for the reader in a hurry? If you wrote a letter, does your first paragraph contain a short summarising sentence, telling the reader in a little more detail than the heading can, what the letter is going to be about? There will be more about the value of summaries on Friday.

If you collected five pluses, you did very well. Four is good. Three is an average score. Less than this and you should learn several useful things from this book.

Quantitative analysis

Carry out the five tasks below.

- Count the number of words you have written (excluding the title and any headings). You can learn something from this alone which may be useful and we shall see what this is in the next section.
- Count the number of sentences. Remember a sentence ends with a full stop; colons and semi-colons (like that one) do not count.

- Count the number of long words. You should count all words which have more than two syllables or sound segments. You can, however, exclude from the count proper nouns (words which would normally begin with a capital letter), words which are combinations of shorter, simpler words (e.g., overlooking, undertaking, roundabout, countryside) and words where the third and last syllable is -es or -ed (e.g., services, expected).
- Calculate the average sentence length (the number of words divided by the number of sentences).
- Calculate % of long words (the number of long words divided by the total number of words multiplied by 100).

Now, after all that hard work, let us see what this information can tell us about our writing.

What these tell us

Each of these pieces of information can tell us something useful about out writing. We can also use the last two to calculate a further piece of information which it is useful to have, as we shall see shortly.

Number of words
This tells us something about our production rate when writing. Most of us when we are calculating the length of a piece of writing tend to talk in terms of pages written. Clearly, this is a very imprecise measure.

The amount produced will depend on:

- the size of the page
- the number of lines
- the size of our handwriting (or the typeface if we are working on a word processor)

Many professional writers measure quantity in words rather than pages. This is because editors will ask for, say, an article of 1000 words. Publishers will ask for a book of 60,000 words, and so on. It is a more exact measurement of quantity.

When might you want to know the word count?

When:

- you wish to manage your time more effectively
- you wish to estimate total writing time
- you wish to set realistic deadlines for writing tasks of various kinds
- you wish to complete a piece of writing more quickly as well as more effectively

If you wish to manage your time more effectively, it is useful to have some idea of how long a writing task will take.

Suppose, for instance, you have a report to write and you know from experience that it is likely to take you about an hour. Suppose further that you have only half an hour before your next meeting, appointment or lunch. The question then arises: Is this a good time to start?

What is going to happen? You will get half way through and have to leave off. What happens next? When you come back to the task later, you will have to go over what you have already written to put yourself back in the picture. This is not good time management.

Far better, where you can, to put the right-sized activities into the right-sized time slots. You cannot always achieve this because life is not neat. Where you can, it is a great help.

Number of sentences
This tells us whether we tend to write in short sentences or long ones. The significance of this will become clear shortly.

Number of long words
This tells us whether or not we have a preference for long words rather than shorter ones or whether we are using jargon terms or not. The significance of this will also become clear shortly.

Average sentence length
The average sentence length should be less than 20 words. If it is higher than this, you could have a problem. You do not inevitably have a problem, but research indicates that readers misread longer sentences, and therefore misunderstand them, more often than shorter ones.

Proportion of long words

The percentage of long words should be less than 10%. Again, research indicates that the higher the proportion of long words, the more likely the material is to be misunderstood.

The Fog Index

What is the Fog Index? It is a measure of how prone your writing is to being 'foggy', that is, lacking in clarity. It is not a precise measure, but it can have its uses.

How do you calculate it? Like this:

Add the average sentence length to the % of long words and multiply by 0.4.

Example:
Average sentence length = 20
% long words = 10

Fog Index = 0.4(20+10)=12

According to research, the figure you finish with is roughly equivalent to the number of years of full-time education someone will need to have had in order to read what you have written with reasonable ease and efficiency.

You might like to apply it to some of the letters and reports you have produced recently at work. To take a short cut, rather than count the total number of words in a document, take a sample of 100 words and work it out on that.

It may very well surprise you by how high the figure is, especially on standard letters and standard paragraphs used in reports. For some reason, when people prepare these, they often write to impress rather than express.

Lessons learnt

In the course of this chapter, you have learnt:

- The need for planning what you write before you write it. We shall return to this tomorrow because it is the key to effective writing.
- The need for titles and headings to show the reader where you are going, so that they can more easily follow you.
- The need for proper paragraphing.
- How long it might take you to write something if you can estimate the likely length in advance.
- Whether or not you have a tendency to write too many long sentences.
- Whether or not you have a tendency to use too many long words or too much jargon.
- What your average sentence length is.
- What percentage of long words you use.
- The level of your Fog Index resulting from the last two pieces of information.

The WRITER'S Strategy – Work, Recitation, Incubation, Treatment

Now that we know a little more about how we write at the moment, we need to know how we should change our approach to make our writing clearer and more effective. We need a strategy, a systematic approach that will help us to improve our writing skills no matter what it is that we are seeking to produce: letter, memo, report, proposal or any other type of business document.

The approach you will learn in the next three days I have called 'The WRITER'S Strategy'. The mnemonic name comes from the seven stages in the strategy, which are:

The WRITER'S Strategy

- **W**ork, or the collection of information for the document you are preparing.
- **R**ecitation, or the storing of the information you have collected.
- **I**ncubation, or a pause between stages.
- **T**reatment, or producing a planned structure.
- **E**xecution, or the actual writing of the document.
- **R**evision, or editing and polishing the document.
- **S**ubmission, or giving or sending the document to the intended reader or readers.

Today, we shall cover the first four stages, but before you begin to collect any information, there are three things you need to know:

- what you are writing about
- who you are writing for
- why you are writing

It is worth writing these three things down in a single sentence each. It helps to clarify the mind and will ensure that you do not wander from the point. You might even write them on cards and place them where you can see them as you work. This will guarantee that you never lose sight of your subject, your readership and your purpose.

Work

Sometimes, the work involved in collecting information together for a piece of writing is minimal, as, say, in preparing a note for the milkman. At other times, for instance for a lengthy report, it may be quite considerable and take several weeks or even months to assemble. How you collect it and where you collect it from may vary from one occasion to another.

- Sometimes you acquire your information from other sources, like previously written reports, or handbooks or works of reference.
- Sometimes you collect it by attending meetings or making visits or interviewing people.
- Sometimes you collect it by carrying out various forms of work, such as tests or experiments or other tasks.
- Sometimes you may already have all the information you need in your head.

Only you can decide which is the most appropriate method in each case. This is another reason why you need to be particularly clear in your own mind about what it is you are writing, for whom and why.

Whichever methods you decide to use, there are two simple techniques that you might find useful, if you do not use them already. They are known by various names. Here, we shall call them:

- the journalist's questions
- the recall tree

Research into the ways in which effective writers work has shown that these techniques are very useful in:

- making sure that no important aspect of a subject is overlooked
- helping to make a writer's life much easier and more productive when it comes to deciding on the treatment to give the subject

These techniques are the basis of the Recitation stage of the WRITER'S Strategy.

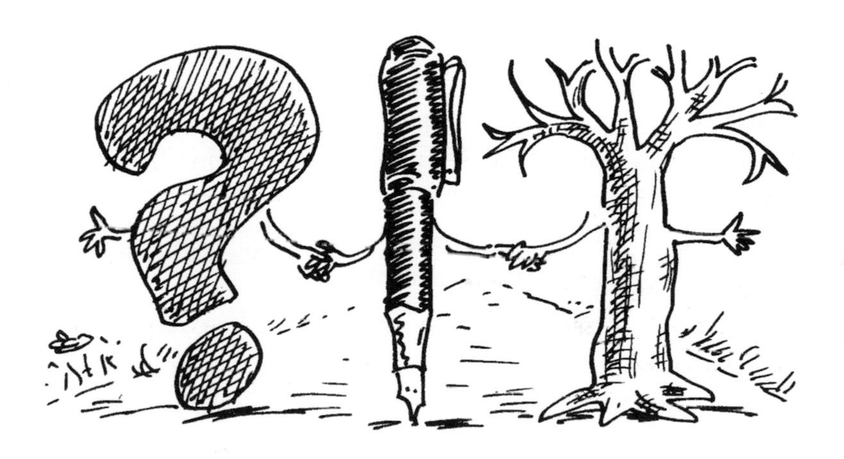

Recitation

Once you have collected all the information you need, you have to store it in a convenient form. The two techniques I have just mentioned will help you to do this.

The first, then, consists of the journalist's questions and these are, quite simply:

- What?
- Why?
- When?
- How?
- Where?
- Who?

They are useful to a writer because they cover all the angles. When you ask the question 'What?' you are automatically looking for information about events, actions or things. Ask 'Why?' and you are looking for reasons, conclusions, deductions, inferences, implications or opinions. Ask 'When?' and you are looking for information about time. Ask 'How?' and you obtain information about method or methods or processes. Ask 'Where?' and you get information about place or location, and ask 'Who?' and information about people is produced.

The second technique is the recall tree. This is essentially an alternative method of making notes to the one that most people use. The most popular method is to make lists of the facts or the points you will make. Now, lists are very useful, but they do suffer from at least two disadvantages.

- First, there is always a tendency to regard the higher items on the list as being more important than the ones lower down.
- Second, the more items there are in the list, the more difficult it becomes to see interrelationships between different pieces of information.

The recall tree overcomes problems like these by, instead of starting at the top of the page as you do with a list, beginning in the middle. There is an example of a recall tree overleaf.

If you have not used these techniques before, try them the next time you have to write something and see if you find them useful. They can also be used for other purposes, such as:

- self-testing when you want to see how much you know about a subject
- making decisions; they can be a useful alternative to lists of advantages and disadvantages
- solving problems

Incubation

When all the information you need, or can reasonably acquire in the time available, is to hand it is a good idea to have a break. You need a little time to let things mull over in the mind and allow for further thoughts to emerge. This is not always possible during a busy day at work, but it is still worth looking for opportunities for periodic breaks between the various stages of a task. They enable you to come back to what you were doing and look at matters with a fresh eye or to look at them as if someone else had done them.

Often, you do not need to create time artificially for incubation periods, but can use some of life's natural breaks,

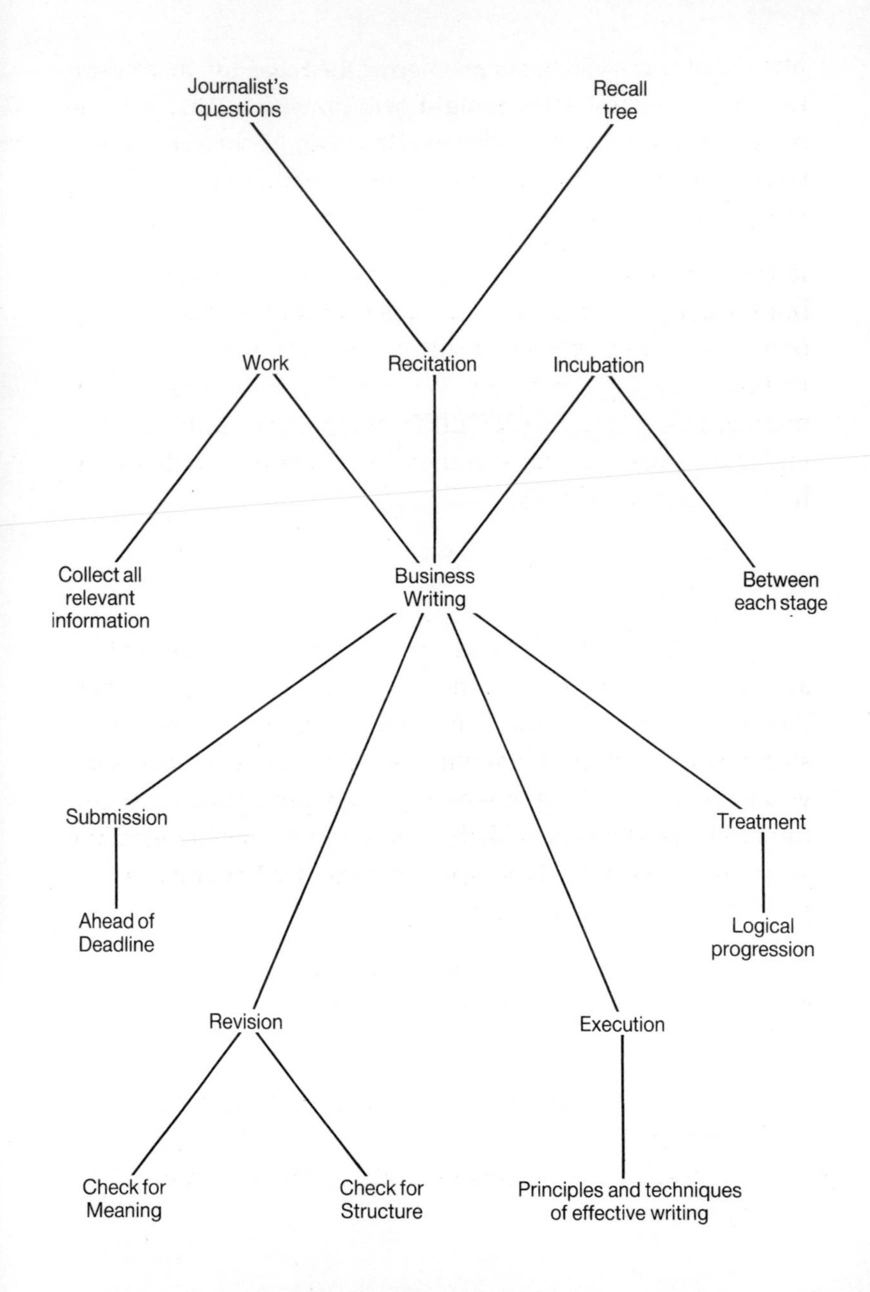
Journalist's questions
Recall tree
Work
Recitation
Incubation
Collect all relevant information
Business Writing
Between each stage
Submission
Treatment
Ahead of Deadline
Logical progression
Revision
Execution
Check for Meaning
Check for Structure
Principles and techniques of effective writing

like meetings, making phone calls, coffee and lunch breaks and so on. Ideally, an overnight break is best so that you can really clear your mind and you should do this when something is important. For everyday writing tasks, a few minutes attending to something else should be sufficient.

In the WRITER'S Strategy, incubation only appears once, but you should remember that it is useful to take a break between each stage when writing. I did not put all the incubation periods in simply because, if you do, the mnemonic becomes WIRITIEIRIS, which sounds like some kind of disease! I am sure you will see the point without my have to insert all the 'I's.

Treatment

This is the key stage. Get this right and the document will almost write itself. Yet it is the stage that most people either pay insufficient attention to or omit altogether and simply start writing. The problem with doing that, of course, is that you have no clear idea of where you are going until you get there. The reader is also likely to have problems in following your line of thought. Time spent planning what you are going to do is never wasted.

You have to remember the relative roles of writer and reader in the process of communication:

- the writer's role is one of synthesis; putting things together
- the reader's role is one of analysis; taking things apart

It will clearly be much harder for the reader to take what they need from your material or what you want them to have if they cannot easily see how you have structured it.

In determining the treatment you will give your subject, there are questions you need to answer:

Deciding the treatment

- Of the information you have collected, how much will you use?
- What, precisely, will you discard?
- What does the reader **need** to know?
- How many sections does your information break into? (These would simply be paragraphs in a letter, for example; in a report, they would be sections. We shall return to planning these kinds of documents more specifically on Thursday and Friday.)
- On what logical basis will your material be organised? (We shall look at some of the possibilities with an example in the next four pages.)
- Will the reader be able to see a logical progression through the material?

Always remember that your treatment is your structure. Without it, you may ramble and repeat yourself.

Since the treatment (or plan) is the key to success in writing, it will be useful to have a little exercise in planning. Here are some complaints made by passengers about railway services (not necessarily British Rail, of course!). Arrange the items in sections under appropriate headings. Do this before you look at the next section to see how your treatment compares with mine.

Complaints about rail services

- not enough space for luggage on train
- long queues at travel centres
- too few luggage trolleys on stations
- luggage trolleys had defective wheels
- trains were delayed
- trains were overcrowded
- luggage trolleys too small for large cases
- no one around to answer information queries
- station buffets were closed too early at night

- waiting rooms were too small
- seats on trains too narrow and too close together
- could not hear station announcements clearly
- air-conditioning on trains either too hot or too cold
- buffet cars on trains sometimes not open during journey
- buffet cars close too soon before end of journey
- staff not helpful or polite when asked questions
- trains made unscheduled stops
- no seats on platforms
- menus not changed often enough in train restaurant cars
- could not get information from local stations

A suggested treatment

1 Introduction

Purpose of writing

2 Quality of customer service on trains

2.1 Trains were delayed.
2.2 Trains made unscheduled stops.
2.3 Trains were overcrowded.
2.4 Seats on trains too narrow and close together.
2.5 Air-conditioning on trains either too hot or too cold.

3 Quality of customer service at station

3.1 Long queues at travel centres.
3.2 Waiting rooms were too small.
3.3 No seats on platforms.

4 Information services

4.1 Could not get information from local stations.
4.2 Could not hear station announcements clearly.
4.3 No one around to answer information queries.
4.4 Staff not helpful or polite when asked questions.

5 Luggage handling

5.1 Not enough space for luggage on train.
5.2 Too few luggage trolleys on stations.
5.3 Luggage trolleys had defective wheels.
5.4 Luggage trolleys too small for large cases.

6 Catering

6.1 Station buffets were closed too early at night.
6.2 Buffet cars on trains sometimes not open during journey.
6.3 Buffet cars close too soon before end of journey.
6.4 Menus not changed often enough in train restaurant cars.

7 Conclusion

There are faults here that need to be remedied.
Request to be kept informed of action taken.

I have chosen to group the items under areas of importance as I see them and then have set out the sections in the order of descending importance, in which the most important area comes first and the least important last. You may well have chosen a different method. This does not mean that you will have done it wrongly. There is no such thing as the perfect plan, but you can use the structure to place emphasis where you want it to be.

There are several other methods of logically ordering information which you could have used. Some of these are:

- Order of ascending importance, in which the most important point comes last. This is more usual for oral statements than for written ones, which tend to use the order of descending importance.
- Order of encounter, or chronological order, in which you deal with things as you come across them.
- Order of volume of items. Here it would be the section with the most complaints which would come first and the one with the least would come last.
- Order of area of concern. This would be suitable where the sections into which information is split are all of more or less equal importance.
- Moving from general matters to more specific ones.
- Moving from specific examples to making more general statements.

- Order of how matters will be sent out for action. To use this here we should need to know more about how the rail service in question is organised.
- Order of personal preferences. This would give us the loosest of logical structures, but could be suitable for some documents. In this example, you might have put catering first if you were always hungry or thirsty when you travelled.

Lessons learnt

In the course of this chapter, you have learnt:

- The need for a systematic approach to writing.
- The first four stages of the WRITER'S Strategy.
- Some of the main ways in which you can collect information.
- How to use the journalist's questions to ensure that you have not overlooked any important aspect of your subject.
- How to use the recall tree to store information in a form which makes planning easier.
- The need for incubation periods between stages in writing where time permits.
- The treatment or plan you select for your material is the key stage in writing.
- A checklist for deciding the treatment to use.
- Some of the logical sequences in which you can deal with material, depending on where you wish to place emphasis.

The WRITER'S Strategy – Execution

We come now to the stage which most people dread: the execution or writing stage. It is now that we have to put our information and ideas into words. This is the stage that you may think will cause you the most problems. If you have carried out the work, recitation and treatment stages properly, with incubation periods between each one, many problems which might arise simply will not.

We can avoid most difficulties by knowing:

- how to approach the actual writing
- the principles and techniques of effective writing
- practical tips for effective writing
- alternatives to long words and phrases

These are some of the things we shall learn today and they will make it even less likely that we shall have problems with our writing.

How to approach the actual writing

Many people work quite slowly when they are writing. They proceed sentence by sentence and paragraph by paragraph trying to get everything right as they go along. This approach suffers from at least two serious disadvantages:

- it is slow
- until you get to the end, you are always working with an incomplete context

It is slow for fairly obvious reasons. You are continually stopping to read over what you have just written and see how it fits in with what you wrote earlier.

You are always working with an incomplete context because you can only see what is down on paper. The rest is still inside your head. This makes it very difficult, if not impossible to see the effects of a change on what is yet to come. For this reason, if for no other, it offers a very ineffective method of writing.

It is far better to work quickly and to regard what you put down as a first draft only. You will have the opportunity to make changes during the revision stage, which we shall come to tomorrow. Because you will then have a complete context to view, you will be able to see the effects of changes on both what precedes and what follows. In the event, if you have indeed carried out the earlier stages properly, there will probably not be much need to make many changes.

Wherever possible, you should try to write whatever it is you are writing at a single sitting. This way, you are much more likely to have the same concept in mind of what you are trying to achieve when you finish as you had when you started out. The longer the period of time over which you write something, the greater the danger that you will, perhaps slightly, but significantly, change your mind. This confusion on your part will almost inevitably be transmitted to the mind of the reader.

To achieve a shorter writing time, it is useful to set a deadline by when you want to finish. Deadlines concentrate the mind, even if you do not keep rigidly to them.

The principles and techniques of effective writing

There is a big temptation when you are writing to seek to impress your readers rather than simply to express clearly and concisely what you have to say. For this reason, you need to give your readers space – literally by not cramming everything into the shortest possible amount of paper – but also in the way you write. So, to be effective, you need SPACE:

SPACE

- **S**implicity
- **P**ositiveness
- **A**ctive voice
- **C**onciseness
- **E**ffectiveness

Let us look in a little more detail at each of these and the contribution they can make to your writing.

Simplicity

There is no point in making matters more complicated than they already are. You have to remember that most people are not particularly quick readers. Nor do they take in everything you tell them. Research shows that the average reader reads most things for most purposes at speeds of about 150–250 words per minute. This compares with a reading aloud speed of about 120–150 words per minute.

When tested on what they have read, their comprehension level is on average around 70–75%. Thus, anything that you do to make life more difficult for them is likely to slow them down even more and make them understand less. Since you usually want more from your readers than they want from you, you do yourself no favours.

Keep your message as simple as you can without oversimplifying. Readers who can understand what you tell them are more likely to respond as you want them to than those who do not.

Positiveness
Research has shown that readers find positive statements easier to understand than negative ones.

- Positive: It is reasonable to believe that this solution will work.
- Negative: It is not unreasonable to believe that this solution will work.

Apparently, by measuring brain activity when people were reading, researchers discovered that readers had to work harder when processing negative statements than they did when processing positive ones. They were also more likely to misunderstand them, possibly as a consequence of having to work harder.

Active voice
Researchers also found that when you write things in the active voice they are easier to read than when they are written in the passive voice. That sentence begins in the active voice and then moves into the passive. In case you are unclear about the difference, as many people are, here is another example:

- Active voice: I sent you an invitation.
- Passive voice: An invitation was sent to you by me.

As you can see, word order in the passive voice is almost the reverse of the order in the active voice. The passive form is usually longer as well. Naturally, longer statements take longer to read and, as we have seen, the reader is more likely to misunderstand them.

Conciseness

There is little to gain by putting information in documents simply because you have gone to the trouble to find it out. Everything that is there should be there because the reader needs to know it.

This applies all the way through, even down to the level of the sentence. It means that you should take pains to eliminate unnecessary words from sentences, like this:

- We have introduced several new innovations as an essential prerequisite of our planned strategy for success and achievement of goals in the single market.

This could quite simply be:

- We have introduced several innovations essential to our strategy for success in the single market.

Effectiveness
This is the result of doing no more after reading this book than following these four principles. Hopefully, by the time you reach Saturday, you will have encountered many more techniques to improve your writing skills.

Incidentally, if you follow these principles, your writing will be more persuasive. Readers are more likely to accept what you tell them if they find your material easy and pleasant to read. We shall return to this point when considering proposals on page 86.

Practical tips for effective writing

You will make your writing more effective if, in addition to remembering what you have read already, you take account of the following tips.

- Be aware of types of writing. It can help you to stay in control and keep to the point if you know which type of writing you are producing. There are only four types:

- description
- exposition
- argument
- narrative

Description Here, you seek to use words to create a picture in the reader's mind.

Example: The beer is a rich golden brown and has a deep creamy head when poured into a measured pint glass, just like well-tended draught beer.

Exposition In this type of writing, you give information or explain something.

Example: The effect is achieved by using our new patented draught-flow system in each can.

Argument In this, you make a case, analyse or refute a proposition, give opinions or put forward a justification.

Example: The taste is very close to that of draught beer and we think that most people will prefer it to the traditional rather fizzy taste of normal canned beer.

Narrative Here, you are essentially telling a story, as you give information or make points in chronological order.

Example: For the best result, you lift the tab on the top of the can and pour the contents directly into the centre of an upright glass.

Most of the time, these types will be mixed in a piece of writing, but one will usually dominate and if you are aware of the dominant type you are using, it helps you to keep to the points you wish to make.

- Leave out qualifying phrases and statements unless they are essential to the meaning. The clearer a run you can give a reader at the subject, the better for them.

Qualifications make your sentences longer and more complex, with all the disadvantages that brings for readers.

Example: The result, though this may not always be the case, may be that you confuse the reader.

This might be better as, simply;

Example: The result may be that you confuse the reader.

The word 'may' covers the possibility that this may not always be the case.

- Make sure that you know the meanings of words and use them appropriately. Avoid jargon.

Example: We shall have to interface to discuss this problem.

Here, a jargon term 'interface' is used inappropriately. The sentence would be better as:

Example: We shall have to meet to discuss this problem.

- Make sure that each sentence deals with a single point and each paragraph with a single topic.

Example: Sales figures for the current quarter are lower than for the same period last year and there has been some ill-feeling generated amongst the staff by the car parking problem.

I think I can leave you to spot what is wrong with this sentence.

We might finish this part of today's work by briefly noting some other pieces of advice traditionally given to writers. Most of them are common sense, but they are still often overlooked. I have written each one so that it is actually a demonstration of the fault you should avoid. I make no claim to authorship of them. They have been around in the 'trade' for many years. If anyone knows who first used them, or knows of a similar list, I should like to know. Write to me care of the publishers.

- Avoid run-on sentences they are hard to read.
- Do not use no double negatives.
- Verbs has to agree with their subjects.
- No sentence fragments.
- Proofread carefully to see if you any words out.
- Avoid commas, that are not necessary.
- If you reread your work, you will find on rereading that a great deal of repetition can be avoided by rereading and editing.

- A writer must not shift your point of view. (This one confuses some people. They say, 'Why not? That's what writers are supposed to do – persuade you to change your mind'. But that is not what is meant here. The viewpoint has been changed. To be correct, the sentence should read either, 'A writer must not shift his or her point of view' or 'When writing, you must not shift your point of view.' If you do, it produces precisely the kind of confusion that the sentence in its present form produces.)
- Do not overuse exclamation marks!!!
- Place pronouns as close as possible, especially in long sentences of 30 or more words, to their antecedents.
- Hyphenate between syllables when breaking a word over two lines and avoid un-necessary hyphens.
- Don't use contractions like don't in formal writing.
- Writing carefully, unrelated participles must be avoided.
- It is incumbent upon us to avoid archaic words.
- Everyone should be careful to use a singular pronoun with singular nouns in their writing.
- Also, avoid awkward or affected alliteration.
- "Avoid overuse of 'quotation "marks"'."
- Last but not least, avoid clichés like the plague; seek viable alternatives.

Alternatives to long words and phrases

Sometimes it is better to use a long word if it will replace several shorter ones. It may, for instance, be better to put 'unnecessarily' instead of 'without the need for'. Usually, though, your writing will be more concise and clearer, and therefore more effective, if you use shorter words and phrases when you can. Some examples of the possibilities are listed below:

Long words and phrases	**Shorter alternatives**
conclusion	end
extraordinary	strange
purchase	buy
inculcate	teach
commence	begin
indisposed	ill
debilitated	weak
magnitude	size

<table>
<tr><td>utilise</td><td>use</td></tr>
<tr><td>facilitate</td><td>help</td></tr>
<tr><td>wholly unfounded</td><td>not true</td></tr>
<tr><td>I have endeavoured to ascertain</td><td>I have tried to find out</td></tr>
<tr><td>due to the fact that</td><td>because</td></tr>
<tr><td>on the occasion of</td><td>when/on</td></tr>
<tr><td>in the event that</td><td>if</td></tr>
<tr><td>with regard to</td><td>about</td></tr>
<tr><td>in recognition of the fact that</td><td>as</td></tr>
<tr><td>with a view to</td><td>to</td></tr>
<tr><td>enclosed herewith</td><td>here is</td></tr>
<tr><td>attached please find</td><td>I enclose</td></tr>
<tr><td>up to the present time</td><td>till now</td></tr>
<tr><td>please do not hesitate</td><td>please</td></tr>
<tr><td>awaiting the favour of your reply</td><td>I should be glad to hear from you</td></tr>
<tr><td>if I can be of any further assistance</td><td>if I can give you any more help</td></tr>
<tr><td>at your earliest convenience</td><td>as soon as you can</td></tr>
<tr><td>furnish all necessary particulars</td><td>give full details</td></tr>
</table>

Lessons learnt

In the course of this chapter, you have learnt:

- How to approach the task of actually writing a document.
- The advantage of producing a first draft.
- The importance of writing things at a single sitting when you can.
- The benefit of setting deadlines.
- The need to give your reader SPACE – simplicity, positiveness, the active voice, conciseness and thereby achieve effectiveness.
- The characteristics of the four types of writing – description, exposition, argument and narrative.
- The principles and techniques of effective writing.
- Practical tips for effective writing.
- Alternatives to long words and phrases.

The WRITER'S Strategy – Revision, Submission

Once you have written something, that is not the end of the matter. Indeed, you could say that you still have to go through a very important stage. Careful revision is essential if you are to be sure that your material is of the highest quality of which you are capable.

Time pressures may limit how much revising you can do, but you should always do as much as you can. Today we shall examine a method of achieving this as easily and as quickly as possible. More specifically, we shall learn:

The final stage
- the importance of the incubation period at this point
- how to edit to achieve the best effect
- what to check for
- checking for the most common errors
- how to use layout to increase readability

These will enable us to put right any faults that may still remain in what we have written. We shall be able to submit our material to our readers confident that we have done everything we can to make the experience of reading it as pleasant and productive as possible.

The most important incubation period

You will recall that, although it only appears once in the mnemonic title of the WRITER'S Strategy, an incubation period is useful between all stages. Nowhere is this more true than now. It is essential that, before you check what you have written, you detach yourself from it.

There is little point in checking something as soon as you have written it for the simple reason that you are too close to it. Whatever you do at work, you give it your best shot, do you not? There is not much to be gained from shoddy workmanship. This means that if you check something as soon as you have finished doing it, the chances are that you will conclude that there is not much wrong with it. After all, you have only just done it and you do not deliberately do things wrongly.

Have you ever written a letter of complaint and left it overnight before sending it? What do you do the following day? You nearly always tone it down a little, do you not? Having got things off your chest, you now try to make your points with a little more reason and a little less abuse. People do not respond well to abuse. Your letter will simply find its way into the nearest bin if it is too abusive.

How to edit

You will need to check your work at least twice if you are to do it effectively. You will need to check that it says what you want it to say in the way you want to say it. You will also need to check that all the technicalities of expression – the structure, the layout, grammar, punctuation and spelling and so on – are as correct as you can make them.

What to check for

The following two checklists will be helpful in enabling you to edit and check effectively.

Checking the meaning

- Have you repeated yourself without good reason?
- Does each paragraph deal with a separate topic?
- Can any paragraphs be removed without loss of meaning?
- Have you omitted any important details?
- Are any statements ambiguous?
- Have you kept your readers in mind and written for them?
- Does the piece read smoothly and is there a logical progression in the points you make?
- If there is a title and if there are headings, do they accurately describe what follows?
- Will the readers understand what the piece is about, who it is for and why you have written it?
- Do any statements contradict each other?
- Will the reader see clearly what is fact and what is opinion?

- Do the facts clearly justify all conclusions drawn and, if present, recommendations made?
- Have you checked the readability of the document?
- Can any words, phrases, or sentences be removed without loss of meaning?
- If you received this document, would you know exactly how to respond to it?
- Would any of the information be better in the form of a diagram, table, chart or other visual medium?
- Would it be desirable, if time permits, to have another incubation period and to check the material again?

Checking the technicalities of expression

- Have you followed the principles and techniques of effective writing?
- Have you avoided jargon as far as possible?
- Is each paragraph in its proper place?
- If you have written a report or similar document, is there any information that you should take out and put into an appendix?
- Have you checked the grammar, punctuation and spelling?
- Is the layout attractive to the eye?
- If the material is typewritten, are there any typographical errors?
- Are you completely satisfied with the piece? Even if you are and if time permits, check it again.

Other points to consider

Using the two checklists above should help you to spot most of the errors and deficiencies you need to find, but there are some further general and, indeed, more specific points to watch.

- Have you, or can you get, a typewritten draft to work with? It makes checking much easier if you can. Many people in business these days have acquired at least rudimentary keyboard skills as a result of using computers. I cannot touch type and I only use first and second fingers of each hand, with thumbs for the space bar, but I can still type faster than I can write longhand. The result is infinitely more legible than my handwriting. I strongly recommend that you consider typing if you can. One other advantage is that you can more easily set out the document as you wish to see it.

- Does your organisation have a style manual or a house style that everybody follows? If it does, make sure you are familiar with it. Readers tend to prefer it if similar documents follow a similar style. It makes it easier and quicker to find what they are looking for.

- Avoid abbreviations and initials if you can. If you have to use them, make sure that you write the term out in full the first time you use it with the initials following in brackets, like this: Greenwich Mean Time (GMT).
- Numbers are normally written out in words unless they are dates, amounts of money, percentages or other statistics, for example:

Write: There are three possible solutions to this problem.

Do not write: There are 3 possible solutions to this problem.

- It is usual nowadays to use single rather than double quotation marks for direct speech, for example:

The Managing Director said, 'We have had a good year'.

Common errors

So that you can see how good you are at identifying errors in statements, try this little exercise. Correct the following sentences where you think it is necessary. Just to make it more of a challenge, some sentences may not contain any errors at all. You will find the answers on page 95.

1 There's too many people in this office.
2 Their not going to achieve their targets this year.
3 They're having there meeting at four o'clock.
4 Its not going to work.
5 The company has improved it's performance this quarter.
6 I have nothing to wear for the office party.
7 Where you there when the accident happened?
8 She has a most irritating manner when talking to superiors.
9 The results of the test is eagerly awaited.
10 Neither the manager or the foreman could solve the dispute.
11 The case against relocation has been literally demolished.
12 Every one of the workers were reluctant to work overtime.
13 This is the man who I saw stealing the equipment.
14 The member of staff which lost the file was reprimanded.
15 The managing director said he is not going to be in the office tomorrow.
16 These kind of problems are difficult to solve.
17 We find ourselves offered a fairly unique opportunity.
18 The amount of industrial accidents is a cause for concern.
19 When you are hoping for promotion, one should work hard.

20 The machine was continuously breaking down.
21 We must try and find a solution to the problem.
22 The man was payed a good wage for his work.
23 He was not able to attend neither of the meetings.
24 She said it would be alright to wait.
25 I should be pleased if you would attend this conference in my place.
26 You shall find the hotel next to the civic centre.
27 This is an entirely different situation than the one you are talking about.
28 If he had been there, I would see him.
29 Neither of us has any chance of winning.
30 George's father said he would have to find a job on leaving school.

Layout

- Leave generous margins – at least 2.5 cm.
- Use a readable typeface – at least 10 pt. (like this).
- Follow the house style manual, if there is one.
- Begin new sections (in reports, for instance) on a new page.

Submission

Once you have checked your writing as carefully and as thoroughly as you can in the time available, and have considered the layout carefully, you are ready to submit it to your readers.

Lessons learnt

In the course of this chapter, you have learnt:

- The importance of an overnight incubation period, where time permits, between execution or writing and revision.
- How to edit to remove any remaining defects and deficiencies.
- What to check for when you are editing your work.
- A checklist to ensure that the document communicates its meaning clearly.
- A checkist to ensure that the document contains no technical errors in expression and no grammatical, punctuation or spelling errors.

Effective letter writing

Today and tomorrow we shall see how to apply the WRITER'S Strategy specifically to letters and reports, since these are the documents that cause many people the most problems in the daily routine. First, then, let us consider letters.

Much day-to-day business communication takes place in face-to-face encounters or over the telephone. But whenever you have to confirm arrangements and agreements, whenever you have to seek or give detailed information, or whenever you have to convey formal statements of various kinds, you have to write business letters.

Such letters have to be accurate in content, concise in expression and clear in their layout and presentation. Ideally, they should each deal with a single topic or area of concern.

There is another important point you should not overlook. Every letter you send is part of your organisation's public relations. Readers will do more than read the letter. From it, they will obtain an impression of how your organisation sees itself and how it sees those with whom it has to deal. That is why the WRITER'S Strategy should form the basis of your business letter writing. We need, then, to examine:

The WRITER'S Strategy for effective business letters

- Work, Recitation, Incubation and Treatment for letters
- Execution or the writing of letters
- Revision and Submission of letters
- layout of letters

Before we look at each of these as they apply to letters, you should remember the importance in all writing of being as clear as you possibly can about content, readership and purpose.

Remember, before you write, you need to know:

- what you are writing about
- who you are writing for
- why you are writing

Work, Recitation, Incubation and Treatment for letters

Most letters will be less than a page long, so they will not usually contain as much information as a report or a proposal. Nevertheless, you have to check the content and make sure that there are no important omissions.

If you have to deal with more than one subject in the letter, consider whether or not it might be better to write more than one letter. If you have to deal with several topics, consider whether it might help the reader if the paragraphs are numbered.

Recitation for a letter need not consist of much more than key words. All you need is enough to trigger the recall of the points you wish to make when it comes to the writing. You should still find it useful to spend a little time using the journalist's questions and the recall tree that we discussed on Monday.

Incubation is necessary, but because you may have to write several letters in a day, the possibilities for it may be limited. You should still look to using breaks, telephone calls, meetings and the like as opportunities for you to clear your mind of a letter so that you can look at it with a fresh eye when you do come back to it.

The treatment need not be elaborate, but you will still have to decide how many paragraphs you should break your material into and in what order they should appear.

Simple headings will help you to keep track of everything. It is possible to prepare the treatment in your head, but you will find it works better if you have something written down to refer to should you be unlucky enough to get stuck at any point.

Within each paragraph, you need a brief outline of the points to make. Again, key words should provide enough in the way of triggers. There are three formulas for letters that various people have devised, and you might like to consider whether one of them would suit the letter you have to write.

AIDA

Useful for sales letters.

- **A**ttention: catching the reader's attention
- **I**nterest: making the reader curious about what you have to say
- **D**esire: making the reader want what you wish to sell them
- **A**ction: telling the reader what he or she must do

IDCA
A variation on the AIDA theme.

- **I**nterest: catching the reader's attention
- **D**esire: making the reader feel he or she needs your products or services
- **C**onviction: convincing the reader of the soundness of your case
- **A**ction: telling the reader what he or she must do

OFAC
Useful for informative letters.

- **O**ccasion: telling why you are writing
- **F**acts: giving information
- **A**ction: making a request or suggestion or appeal
- **C**losing: offering to provide more information

Execution or the writing of letters

Sometimes you feel execution is indeed the right word to use here, but this stage will have fewer fears if you have completed the previous stages properly and have had an incubation period between each one. As we saw on Tuesday, if you have a carefully-thought-out treatment, documents almost write themselves.

With letters, there are some decisions you have to make at this point which do not always arise with other kinds of writing. For instance, it is particularly important to decide how formal or informal you should be. Will you address your reader by name? Will you use the active voice or the more impersonal and more formal passive voice?

You will need to consider your language and ask if you are using any of the traditional, now rather old-fashioned expressions common in letters. Here are some examples of the kind of writing you should avoid:

Old-fashioned	**Contemporary**
I am in receipt of your letter of...	Thank you for your letter of...
I take great pleasure in confirming that...	I am very pleased to confirm that...
I can assure you that the matter is receiving our active consideration.	I am pursuing this as a matter of urgency.

You may well be able to add many more such phrasings by looking through your own file of the letters people have sent you.

Be courteous and tactful. As we saw earlier, even in letters of complaint, there is little to gain by being abusive. Bearing in mind the public relations function of business letters, there is everything to gain by being polite and pleasant.

With some letters, you may need to consider whether or not the reader will attempt to read between the lines. That is, will they read more in to what you say than is there? If they might, you will have to be especially careful over the choice of words.

Remember that many things are not necessarily best written from beginning to end. If you are having trouble getting started, try writing the body of the letter first. You should then find the opening and the closing easier to write.

Revision and submission of letters

Remember the value of the overnight incubation period before you revise your letter. This is particularly necessary if the letter is a very important one.

Make sure you check the accuracy of your material. In particular:

- Double-check figures, dates, specifications and other details.
- Make sure you have spelled all names correctly (some people can get very upset if you misspell their names).
- Check for any statements which, on reflection, may be a little ambiguous.

- Make sure your letter is neatly typed (it is far better to go to the trouble of typing a letter again rather than sending it out with corrections marked on the text).

One other point that is quite important in business letters is that you should avoid postscripts (PS at the end of a letter). It may show a lack of planning or sloppy thinking and is more likely to irritate the reader than to help him or her.

When it comes to proofreading your letter before final typing, it is worth mastering some of the conventional proofreading marks recommended by the British Standards Institution. Some of the most common ones you might find useful are:

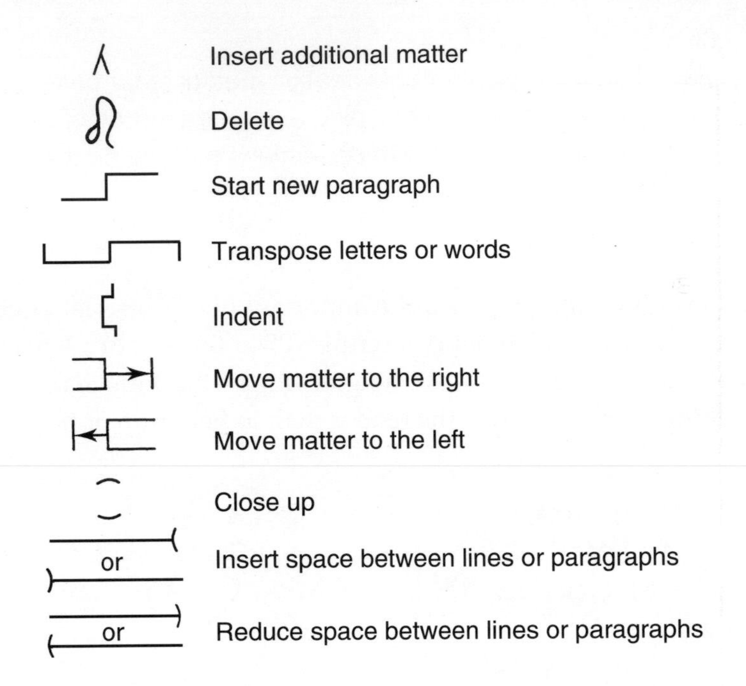

Layout of letters

There are three main kinds of layout in general use:

- block
- semi-block
- indented

Three brief examples will show you the difference:

Block

ABC Promotions Ltd
Enterprise House
European Way
Bridgetown
BW1 9AA

23 May 19--

Dear Mr Robson

Thank you for your enquiry about our products. I enclose a fully-illustrated brochure.

Please contact me personally if you require any further information.

Yours sincerely

G R Wainwright

Semi-block

ABC Promotions Ltd
Enterprise House
European Way
Bridgetown
BW1 9AA

29 May 19--

Dear Mr Robson

Thank you very much for your order. The items you requested have been dispatched today.

Yours sincerely

G R Wainwright

Indented

ABC Promotions Ltd
Enterprise House
European Way
Bridgetown
BW1 9AA

5 June 19--

Dear Mr Robson

    I was delighted to hear how pleased you were with our products and should like to thank you for your second order, which will be dispatched today.
    If there is any further information or assistance you need, please contact me personally.

Yours sincerely

G R Wainwright

Indented is perhaps the least popular style and yet research into readability shows that indented paragraphs are easier and quicker to read than block paragraphs.

If you require more information on some of the more problematical aspects of letter writing, you might find one of my other books useful: *Tricky Business Letters*, published by Pitman, 1993.

Lessons learnt

In the course of this chapter, you have learnt:

- How the WRITER'S Strategy applies to letters.
- The continued importance of incubation periods.
- Three formulas for writing letters.
- Some specific considerations of the use of language when writing letters.
- Old-fashioned expressions to avoid when writing letters.
- Some standard proof correcting marks to use when proofreading letters.
- Some particular points to watch out for when revising letters.
- How to lay out a letter in three different ways.

Effective report writing

It is particularly important when writing reports to have a deadline in mind. Reports, since they are usually longer than letters and consequently involve more work, tend to be put off until the last possible minute. They need to have the traditional time management principle applied to them: do it now.

In fact, it is not at all a bad idea to establish intermediate deadlines for each stage. You might even draw up a small chart like this so that you can see at any point where you are and how far you still have to go:

Stage	W	R	I	T	E	R	S
Complete by:	23/1	2/2	1 day between stages	9/2	18/3	24/3	30/3

Also today, we shall learn:

- special aspects of the WRITER'S Strategy for reports
- the need for extra attention to structuring
- how to write for the non-specialist
- the order of writing the sections of a report
- revision and submission of reports
- readability and legibility factors

Work, recitation, incubation and treatment in reports

For each of the stages in writing there are special factors to keep in mind when preparing reports. There are also additional tips that you should find useful.

Work

You should try to acquire more information about the subject than you will eventually need for the report. This is not to say that you should gather information for the sake of it. The information must be relevant. But it does give you more confidence if you have too much information than if you have too little.

It also means that when you get to the treatment stage you can put yourself into an editing frame of mind as you select what to use. This will carry forward through the remaining stages and increase the chances that you will produce a concise report.

Recitation

This should be more detailed and, indeed, it probably will be simply because reports tend to be longer than other documents produced at work. Remember to use the combination of the journalist's questions and the recall tree. It is not a bad idea to work on blank paper rather than lined paper and to use the paper in landscape style instead of portrait style, like this:

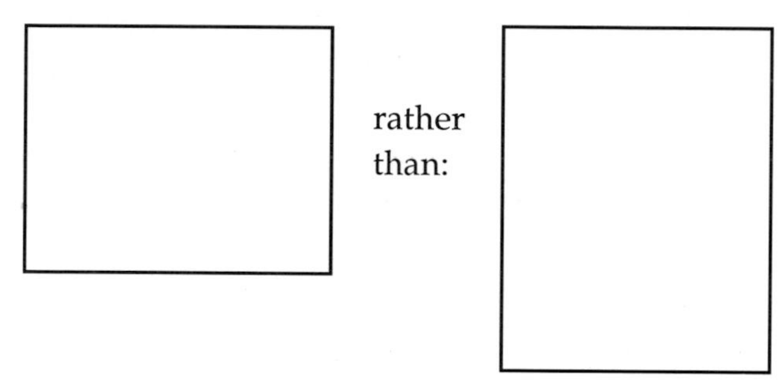

Incubation

Incubation periods should be longer than for letter writing. As a general rule, the longer and more complex a document is, the longer the incubation periods need to be.

Treatment

This may be quite simple or it could become quite complex. The simplest report has three parts:

- Introduction
- Body of report (which would not be called this but would have a heading or headings appropriate to the subject)
- Conclusion

With reports of more than, say, half a dozen pages, you might also have a Summary. This will usually be at the front of the report, for the reader's convenience.

Structuring

If you have a more complex report to write, you might find it useful to have a list of all the possible headings you might need. You will not always need all of them, but you will find that it helps your readers if you always place the ones you do use in the same order. In that way, they will soon learn that, if a heading is not in its usual place, it will not be there at all. This helps them to speed up their processing of your information. For this, they will be grateful.

Parts of a more complex report

- Title page: useful for reports of more than six pages
- Summary: for reports of more than two pages
- Table of contents: for reports of more than six pages
- Introduction: states the purpose
- Body of report (again, using an appropriate heading for each section and **never** using 'body of report' itself as a heading): this is the meat in the pie
- Conclusions: if you have drawn any
- Recommendations: if you have made any
- Acknowledgements: if you have consulted other people
- References: if you have quoted other sources
- Bibliography: if you have referred to books
- Glossary: of terms, abbreviations, symbols, etc.
- Appendices: supplementary information

The sections of a report will be identified by a numbering or lettering system. The most common one in use these days is the decimal system:

1.
    1.1
    1.2
        1.2.1 and so on.

You can also use the American outline system:

I.
    A.
        1.
        2.

    B.
        1.
        2.

II.
    A. and so on.

You can even use a pattern often used by those who do not feel comfortable with either the decimal or the American systems:

A.

   1.

      a)

      b)

   2.

      a)

      b)

B. and so on.

You will probably do best to select the decimal system if you are unsure, simply because this is the most commonly used method.

It is perhaps also worth remembering that if you have both conclusions and recommendations, you have several choices:

- Conclusions and Recommendations all in the one section: best if you do not have many of either
- A separate section for Conclusions and one for Recommendations: best if you have several of each
- Only Conclusions, no Recommendations
- Only Recommendations, no Conclusions
- Neither: as, say, in an accident report where you give the facts and someone else does the interpretation

How to write for the non-specialist

If you are a specialist writing for non-specialist readers, you will need to keep your material, your structure and your language as simple as the subject will allow. The more complex you make things, the more problems your readers will have in understanding what you are trying to tell them.

If you have a great deal of material, it is worth ticking off the points on the recall tree as you use them. In this way, you will be able to see what you have used and decide more easily whether or not you still need the rest.

The order of writing a report

You will find it easier and quicker if you write the body of the report first. It is easier to write an introduction when you can see what you are introducing. It is also easier to write a summary if you write it last. Any other parts of the report you can write in almost any order you choose.

Remember the difference between an introduction and a summary. An introduction states the subject, the purpose and the plan of treatment. It may also contain any essential background information, but, other than this, it will contain no hard facts. The summary, on the other hand, repeats the main points of the report, wherever they are to be found, for the convenience of the reader in a hurry. Good summaries are also useful to all readers as they give them a map of the territory they are about to enter and they can then navigate their way around the report with greater ease and speed.

Should you ever find yourself writing a report as part of a team, try to get everyone to agree on a single person to act as editor. This person's function is simply to see that there is a consistency of structure, style and approach throughout the report. Everyone has their own way of doing things and, if the style varies from section to section, this may confuse the reader. If you cannot agree on an editor, see if you can at least get everyone to agree on a common structure for the report. This will go some way towards preventing readers misunderstanding the text.

Revision and submission of reports

In addition to using what you have already learned about the revision stage, you will find it helps if you can enlist the help of someone else in checking what you have done. You read the report aloud and they follow the text on their copy. You look to see that the report says what you want it to say in the way you want to say it. They check for errors of various kinds.

It might not even matter that the other person does not know much about the subject since they are not checking the content. For this reason, many report writers use their partners to help them do this.

You might wish to use a more sophisticated proofreading system than the one you learned yesterday. If you do, here are some more of the professional proofreader's markings you might consider:

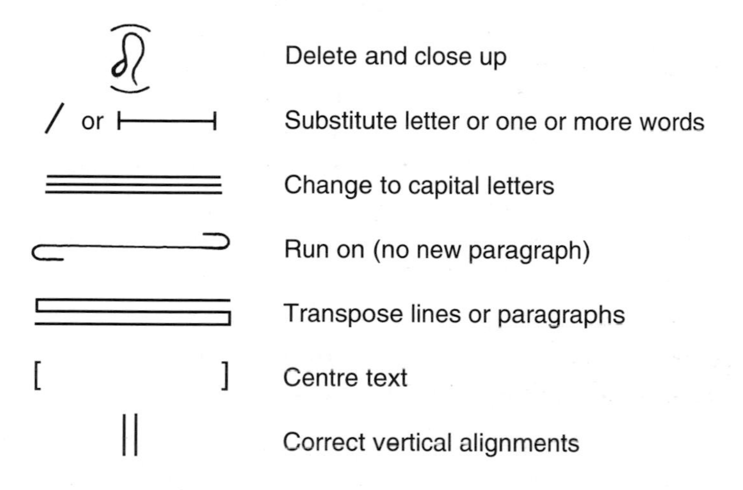

If your report has to be approved by someone else, usually your boss, before it is submitted to its intended readership, it will come back to you with changes. This, of course, you know, but you may have assumed in the past that this was because you had made mistakes. This need not be so. As soon as you put someone in the role of editor, they feel obliged to edit. Remember that we all have our favourite words and phrasings. Remember also that, unless your editor makes some marks, how can you be sure that they have really read it?

Submission
Try to submit ahead of deadline. This will give you a little extra time if you need it and it will impress your boss if you do not. Keep a personal copy so that you can check whether any of those changes I mentioned above have significantly changed your meaning.

Readability and legibility factors

Before you submit your report, you might find it useful to carry out a Fog Index calculation (of the kind we did on Sunday) to assess the level at which you have pitched it. You do not need to base it on the whole report. If you select a sample of 100 words from somewhere near the middle, this will do.

Remember, though, that the Fog Index needs sentences to work with. Lists of bullet points may not work very well or may give you an inaccurate, low figure, making you think you have achieved more than you actually have.

If you type your report yourself or you can specify to the typist how you would like it typed, here are some of the legibility factors which research indicates you should consider if you want to make your reader's life easier:

- Typeface should have serifs (those little embellishments to the basic letter shape, i.e. like the main text of this book); non-serif (called sans-serif i.e. like the text in this box) typefaces take longer to read.
- Italic type is more difficult to read than roman.
- Lower case letters are easier to read than capitals; avoid long headings all in capitals.
- Lines should not be justified (i.e., all ending at the same point as well as beginning at the same point), but left 'right ragged' justified text has uneven spacing between words and poorer readers find it easier if they have even spacing between words.
- Matt paper is preferable to gloss paper, which causes irritating reflections for some readers.
- Ideally, line length should be 5 to 9 cm.
- Type should not be smaller than 10 pt. (this refers to the height of the letters – 72 pts to the inch).
- Indenting the first lines of paragraphs increases speed of reading by 7%.
- Headings should stand out, perhaps by being larger and in a different typeface.
- Tables should be clearly distinguishable from text.
- Arabic numerals are read faster than roman ones.
- Good contrast is needed between paper and print (black print on yellow paper gives the best contrast, but irritates many readers; black print on purple paper gives the worst. Black on white is the best all round choice).

Lessons learnt

In the course of this chapter, you have learnt:

- The desirability of acquiring more information than you will actually need for the report.
- How to structure a report and identify the headings with numbers or letters.
- The order in which to write the various sections to ensure greater speed and effectiveness.
- Points to bear in mind when writing for the non-specialist.
- How to deal with those who have the task of editing and approving your work.
- What to do when writing a report as a member of a team.
- The difference between an Introduction and a Summary.
- More sophisticated proofreading marks.

- The desirability of submitting ahead of deadline.
- The need to keep a personal copy in case others make changes which change your meaning unacceptably.
- The most important aspects of legibility you should take into account when your report is typed.

If you require further guidance on report writing, you should refer to my book, *Report Writing*, published by Management Update, second edition 1990.

Other forms of writing

Before you complete your brief study of some of the techniques that will make your business writing more effective and therefore more successful, we shall look at how you may apply the WRITER'S Strategy to other forms of writing. We shall end with a summary of what you have learned this week.

We shall consider the following today:

- memos
- minutes
- proposals
- CVs
- dictation
- word processing
- computer aids for the writer

Memos

Memos should:

- be as brief as you can make them
- deal with one subject only
- be specific about what you require or what you expect people to do
- state any deadline for action clearly and indicate the degree of urgency for any action required
- be dated and referenced
- be positive rather than negative
- use short numbered points
- be sent only to those who really need them

Minutes

Minutes should contain:

- the date, place and time of the meeting
- the name of the Chair
- the names of those present, unless there are too many to list conveniently, in which case the number attending
- the resolutions passed or rejected by the meeting
- the signature of the Chair obtained at the next meeting to confirm that the minutes are a true record

Ideally, minutes should only record decisions made with the necessary minimum of information on each item. It is best to avoid writing minutes which record everything that was said. Not only does this make the minutes very lengthy, it also increases the scope for error in recording.

The order in which items appear should be the same as on the agenda for the meeting, unless the Chair has taken an item out of sequence or taken two items together. In situations like these, you deal with the items in the minutes as they were dealt with at the meeting.

It helps if you can prepare an outline plan for the minutes before the meeting. If the Chair sticks to the agenda, it may even be possible to write most of the minutes before the meeting takes place. All you will have to do afterwards is insert the decision that was made.

An example of a pre-written item should look like this:

> **Purchase of office equipment**
>
> The Personnel Department has applied to the Board for approval to buy items of office equipment for £10 000. After a full discussion, the application was…

All that needs to be inserted is whether the application was approved or rejected.

One last tip: if you have to write the minutes, sit next to the Chair. You can then quickly clear up any points on which you are doubtful about what the meeting decided.

Proposals

You usually write a proposal because you want money to fund a project or permission to carry out a particular piece of work. Since this means that you will be especially keen to persuade your readers to agree, you should follow the SPACE principles we encountered on Tuesday (pages 36–40).

If you want a positive response from your readers, you do not want to do anything which will produce a negative response. Long words, long sentences, long paragraphs, negative statements and the use of the passive voice are all likely to evoke negative responses from readers. If readers are in a negative frame of mind as a result, you make it less likely that you will get the positive response you want.

Curriculum vitae (CV)

This should preferably consist of a sin
certainly be no more than three. The e
should cover are:

- personal information (full name,
marital status)
- the position you seek or your ca
time
- your relevant experience, worki
recent to the earliest (i.e., in rev
- your education, again in reverse
further than secondary school
- referees (the names and addre
usually three, who have agreed
suitability)
- brief details of hobbies and per

Dictation

If you have to dictate letters and me
have a detailed, point-by-point plan
ramble when you cannot easily see

Above all, practise dictation as muc
before you start to use it at work. A
very helpful for this purpose.

Computer aids

There are several writers' aids available to those who
word processors. None of them offer magic solutions
problems of writing, but most will be helpful tools if
with caution and discretion. The most widely availab
offered by modern word processing packages are:

- a dictionary
- a thesaurus
- a spelling checker
- a grammar checker
- a Fog Index or other readability index
- a word counter
- a facility for producing graphs and cha
- a simple spreadsheet
- a facility for producing templates (layo
be used repeatedly for preparing docu
standard structure)

The one that you need to be particularly c
the grammar checker. No grammar check
context sensitive, so they do sometimes o
advice. I think you are really only safe to
checker if you already have a good groun
grammatical rules and conventions. If yo
would be better off referring to a gramm
consulting a friend or colleague who you
using English.

Lessons learnt

In the course of this chapter, you have learnt:

- How to write memos.
- The best way to tackle minutes of meetings so that you limit the problems that might arise.
- The need to keep proposals positive and to avoid doing anything that will provoke a negative response in the reader's mind.
- How to structure an effective CV.
- How to dictate effectively.
- Factors to consider when selecting a word processor.
- The other computer aids that are available to writers.

You should now be equipped with the skills and knowledge which will enable you to improve both the quality and the speed of your writing.

The week in summary

Here is a handy reference guide to the main topics we have covered this week:

Analysing our writing (Sunday)

- Qualitative analysis
- Quantitative analysis

The WRITER'S Strategy – Work, Recitation, Incubation, Treatment (Monday)

- Methods of collecting information
- The journalist's questions and the recall tree
- The need to pause for reflection after each stage
- The need for a logical structure

The WRITER'S Strategy – Execution (Tuesday)

- The principles and techniques of effective writing
- Practical tips for effective writing

The WRITER'S Strategy – Revision, Submission (Wednesday)

- Checking the meaning
- Checking the technicalities of expression
- Common errors

Effective letter writing (Thursday)

- Formulas for writing letters of various kinds
- Layouts for letters

Effective report writing (Friday)

- Structuring reports
- Readability and legibility factors

Other forms of writing

- Memos, minutes, CVs, and dictation
- Word processing and computer aids for writers

Answers to common errors exercise (pages 55–56)

Nos. 6, 8, 25 and 29 contain no errors.

1 There's should be There are.
2 Their should be They're.
3 there should be their.
4 Its should be It's.
5 it's should be its.
7 Where should be Were.
9 is should be are.
10 or should be nor.
11 Delete literally.
12 were should be was.
13 Delete who (using whom sounds pompous).
14 which should be who.
15 is should be was (reported speech).
16 kind should be kinds.
17 Delete fairly.
18 amount should be number.
19 one should be you.
20 continuously should be continually.
21 and should be to.
22 payed should be paid.
23 neither should be either.
24 alright should be all right.
26 shall should be will.
27 than should be from.
28 see should be have seen.
30 he should be George.